Grandma and Me

Children's Book on Psoriatic Arthritis/Autoimmune Disease

Sue Kleinhuizen

ISBN 979-8-89043-322-0 (hardcover)
ISBN 979-8-89043-323-7 (digital)

Christian Faith Publishing
832 Park Avenue
Meadville, PA 16335
www.christianfaithpublishing.com

Printed in the United States of America

Delilah spends a great deal of time with her grandparents, with Grandma overseeing much of her schooling needs when her parents are busy working. Online learning has become quite popular as a means of getting an education. Delilah's parents chose this style of learning due to the COVID pandemic to decrease her exposure to illnesses. Delilah is an eight-year-old little girl who was diagnosed with psoriatic arthritis at age seven.

Delilah loves her teacher and this style of educational learning. She excels in reading and math and enjoys the fun games and activities she is allowed to try on the computer as she learns. Delilah checked into her daily writing class and had just been given a writing assignment to list the names of her friends, as well as what she had in common with them. Delilah began to cry and expressed to Grandma, "I don't have any friends. All the kids I know are in online learning, and I don't really get to play with them. Even if I could, they probably wouldn't like me."

"Why do you feel that others wouldn't like you?" Grandma asked as she gave Delilah a big hug.

Delilah stated, "Because I have dry patches of skin on my legs, and sometimes my knees and muscles hurt, so I don't run very fast. Maybe they wouldn't want to play with me because I might not be as fast as they are. Or maybe they will be afraid to touch me if they think that they will get dry skin too or get psoriasis. They might think that just because I have psoriatic arthritis, I'm not very smart. I don't think that other kids will understand me." Delilah was developing low self-esteem (how she felt about herself).

The two of them left the computer area to have a private conversation. "First of all," Grandma said, as she wiped away Delilah's tears, "not all your friends need to be your same age. I could be your friend and your grandma. I love you very much just the way you are. Delilah, you are so pretty, kind, intelligent, and caring. Just be comfortable with who you are. Jesus loves everyone just the way we are too. We all are unique and special in our own way.

"Some people are short, and some are tall. Some people have blonde hair, black hair, brown hair, or red hair. My hair is gray. Some wear glasses, and some need braces on their teeth. Some have white skin, and others have dark skin. We are all different and yet very special. People can have different health needs too. What helps is for everyone to understand more about each other and what we can all do to help one another.

"When we treat others with kindness, they will treat us with kindness too. Let's start with your assignment first, and if you think it would be alright, you can write about you and me and what we have in common. Then we will talk to your teacher, and if she agrees, we can make up a presentation about psoriatic arthritis to share with your class." Delilah was delighted with the idea.

What we Have in Common:

Psioriatic Athritis, Crafts, Gardening, Baking, Writing...

The two of them began to make a list of the things they had in common. Grandma reminded Delilah that she too had psoriatic arthritis, and they shared their symptoms with each other. They found that they often get sore muscles from the same things as cold or damp weather. When talking about other things they enjoyed doing, they discovered that many of the fun things they did together were also very special memories for both of them. Delilah found that she did have a good friend and that she had plenty to write about for her assignment. She also felt special because not all grandmas and granddaughters share a special bond as they had. Delilah discovered that she also had a good support system that she could always talk to. A support system is a person or group of people with similar experiences or needs, who can be there for you to show support and comfort.

Delilah and Grandma requested a FaceTime meeting with the teacher to discuss their idea of creating a presentation about psoriatic arthritis to the class. They also wanted to encourage other students to share their physical or mental health needs so the class might become a support system for each other and encourage kindness. The two of them wanted to promote the idea of "When we treat others with kindness, they will treat us with kindness too." The teacher felt that it was a great idea and set a date with Delilah and Grandma to make their presentation. Grandma was a nurse so she knew a lot about their topic, and Delilah was able to provide the kids' perspective on this matter. The two of them started planning their presentation and were very excited to be working together as a team.

Delilah and Grandma decided to make a list of what they felt might be important for Delilah's classmates to know about psoriatic arthritis.

- What is psoriatic arthritis?
- How is this condition diagnosed?
- What are the common symptoms of psoriatic arthritis?
- How do people get psoriatic arthritis? What can trigger it to be worse?
- What are the treatments for this condition?
    - It's important to get enough sleep.
    - It's important to eat a balanced diet.
    - It's important to exercise regularly.
    - It's important to protect your skin.
- What feelings or emotional concerns that a child with psoriatic arthritis may experience?

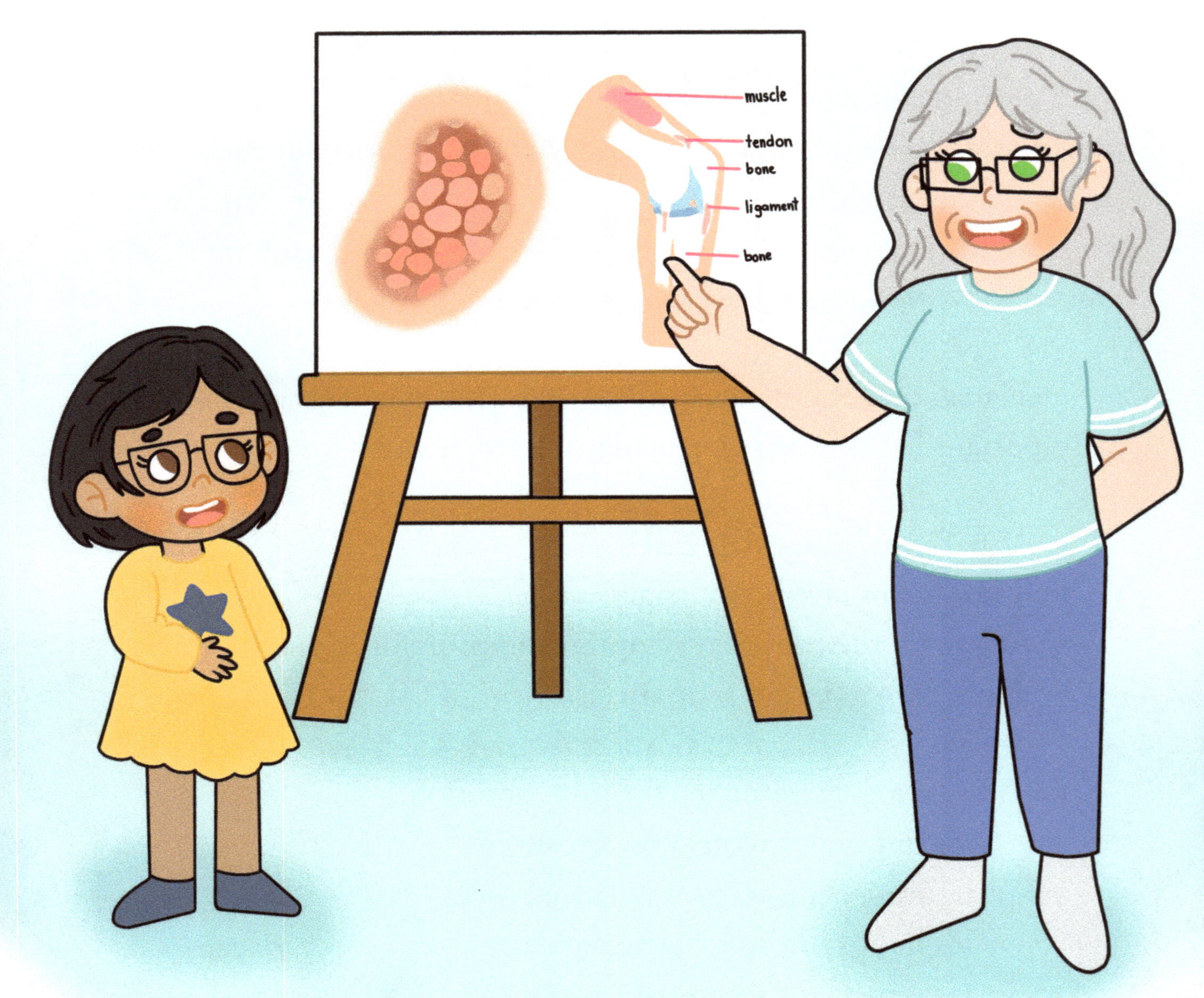

muscle
tendon
bone
ligament
bone

The big day finally arrived and Delilah and Grandma had done their homework. They were able to develop an informative presentation for Delilah's classmates. The two of them had prepared a few illustrations to help present what they had learned.

"What is psoriatic arthritis?

"Psoriatic arthritis is a combination of psoriasis and arthritis. Psoriatic arthritis is an autoimmune disorder. Your immune system is what helps to keep you well and fight off infections or illness. Psoriatic arthritis can happen when our immune system is not working properly.

"Psoriasis (so-ri-a-sis) is a skin condition that may develop dry, scaly, itchy, red- or pink-colored patches on your body. The areas where you are most likely to get these dry skin patches are your knees, elbows, legs, behind your ears, your stomach, back, scalp, or your buttocks. Arthritis affects joints causing inflammation (swelling or stiffness). Joints are places where bones come together that allow your body to bend and move. The joints in your fingers and hands are what allow you to cut with scissors or grip a pencil. Your elbows, shoulders, wrists, knees, hips, and back are other good examples of joints. Riding your bike or running requires you to use many of your joints all at once."

"How is this condition diagnosed?

"Doctors and scientists are still researching this condition to determine what causes it. Doctors believe that it could be hereditary, meaning that it is in your genetics. Genetics are common genes from your parents and family members that often make you look like your mom or dad or a grandma or grandpa or other family members. Genetics can also affect your health or other conditions that you may be more likely to have or develop over time. Sometimes you get health conditions that other family members have, and sometimes you don't.

"My grandma also has psoriatic arthritis and knows other family members with autoimmune disorders. There are no tests that can specifically diagnose psoriatic arthritis, but doctors go by symptoms. You may have more than one doctor that you will see to manage your health. You may see a dermatologist (der-ma-tol-o-gist) and a rheumatologist (roo-muh-tol-uh-jist), along with your pediatrician (pe-di-a-tri-cian). The dermatologist will help to manage your skin or psoriasis, the rheumatologist will help manage arthritis and your joints and muscles, and your pediatrician will manage everything else and at times consult with the other doctors. They will make a diagnosis based on your symptoms, a physical exam, your medical history, your family's medical history, and lab tests or possibly X-rays. The sooner you get medical help, the sooner you will start to feel better and protect your joints from permanent damage. There is no cure for psoriatic arthritis at this time, but doctors and scientists are doing research to learn more about it and to develop newer and better medications to help manage it."

"What are common symptoms?
"Common symptoms include the following:

- joint pain, stiffness, and swelling
- dry patches on your skin or rashes
- fatigue (feeling tired a lot)
- changes in your fingernails or toenails
- redness or swelling in your eyes

Some of the symptoms I have are stiffness in my knees and neck, mostly happening in the mornings. This seems to get better after taking my medications and as I become more active throughout the day. I also get some dry skin patches on my legs, and I have to use a special cream to manage them so the dry areas don't get worse.

"A dermatologist can give helpful hints as to how to manage your skin needs. Taking a short shower with warm water is better for my skin than sitting for a long time in a bathtub with hot water. Heat tends to irritate my psoriasis. For some people, being around chemicals in a swimming pool or hot tub can trigger skin issues. Don't scratch your dry skin areas because it could lead to infections. Pat dry your skin instead of rubbing it hard with a towel.

"I use sunscreen when outside to prevent sunburn. Some sun is good for my skin, but I have to be careful not to get sunburned. I have to use certain shampoos, conditioners, and bodywash, as well as special laundry soap, or my skin becomes itchy, or I get rashes and dry spots.

"Some people can get skin rashes, hives, or dry spots on their body that may appear for a short time and then clear up. Some people can get swollen or puffy joints that swell so badly that it is difficult to use them or bend them. When my joints are stiff, I take my medications and use a warm pack to the affected areas. My body gets tired more easily during those times, and I may need to rest more often. If you have redness and swelling in your eyes, you may need to go to an ophthalmologist (oph-thal-mol-o-gist), a special eye doctor that will monitor the health of your eyes. You may develop some of the symptoms listed above, but it doesn't mean that you would get all of them."

"How do people get psoriatic arthritis / what can trigger it to become worse?

"Psoriatic arthritis can happen when your immune system is not working properly, and it attacks healthy cells and tissues in your body. It appears as though it cannot tell the bad cells from the healthy cells.

When healthy tissues in joints are attacked, it can cause your joints to swell or become inflamed and trigger arthritis. When cells in your skin are affected, it can cause your skin to produce too many skin cells which may result in psoriasis.

"Some things that may trigger this condition may include physical trauma to the body like a serious injury, burns, sunburn, cuts, or a viral or bacterial infection. Stress can also trigger this condition or make the condition worse. If you develop arthritis, it can be affected by cold, damp, or rainy weather, being overweight, or physically overworking your body. My grandma was diagnosed with psoriatic arthritis after breaking her arm badly. She had to have surgery to fix the breaks and had a metal plate implanted in her arm to repair the bones. She had an allergic reaction to the metal and her immune system attacked itself.

"Since your immune system is not working as it should, you are considered to have a weakened immune system. You may be more likely to catch an illness from others around you and may need to be careful to protect yourself from others that may be sick. It may be harder for your body to fight off illnesses if you get what they have. It may be helpful for you to mask or avoid large groups, especially in enclosed areas where it is more likely that illnesses will spread. Wash your hands well with soap and water, for at least twenty seconds, before eating and after handling objects that others have touched. Use hand sanitizers when hot water and soap are not available. Encourage others to cover their mouth and nose when coughing or sneezing, and encourage them to not visit you when they are ill. Being diagnosed with psoriatic arthritis was kind of scary, but learning more about it and how to manage it was helpful."

"What are the treatments for this?

"As we mentioned earlier, your treatment may require a team of health-care professionals or doctors. You may experience what is called a *flare* of your condition, where it may become worse for a short period of time then return to your normal baseline or physical condition (what's normal for you). If the arthritis is difficult to manage, you may also need to see an occupational (oc-cu-pa-tion-al) therapist or a physical therapist. They can help you learn how to adjust to doing things differently or strengthen your muscles so you can return to your normal routine.

"Your doctor may need to do blood tests occasionally to monitor the inflammation (swelling or muscle stiffness) in your body to determine what medications may be necessary to manage your health. Sometimes X-rays are needed to check your joints and tissue health. Treatment depends on how severe your symptoms are. Some people are able to control this illness with medications taken orally (by swallowing a pill, or liquids), and some use creams which are called topical medications (applied to the skin), and some require injections (getting shots). I am able to manage my psoriatic arthritis by taking liquid ibuprofen three times a day and using a warm pack when needed. My grandma needs to take a weekly injection of medication and gives herself her own shots. Exercise and stretches help to maintain good joint health.

"To stay well, eating a balanced diet is important, as well as getting enough sleep and taking care of your skin. Early diagnosis and treatment are important for this diagnosis. Taking your medications and following your doctor's recommendations are also very important. Leaving psoriatic arthritis untreated may increase your symptoms and may lead to long-term disability. Not getting treatment can result in permanent joint damage in as little as six months."

Kids our age need 10-12 hours of sleep

"Sleep is very important for all ages, especially for kids. Our age group should try to get ten to twelve hours of sleep per night. Because our bodies and minds are still growing, we require more sleep than adults. When we sleep, our breathing slows down, our heart beats more slowly, and our brain rests. Our body's cells work on rebuilding and helping to fight off illness. You should try to create a routine of going to bed at the same time each night and waking at the same time each morning. Then it won't be so hard to fall asleep at night. It's better to listen to soft music, read a good book, or have someone read to you than to watch television or play computer games right before bedtime. Some activities make your mind become too active and then you might not be able to relax. Our brains don't work as well if we are tired and fighting to fall asleep in school when we need to be alert and learning. Without enough sleep, our muscles are more tired and unable to help us be as physically active as we would like."

FOOD PYRAMID
for
KIDS
Fats, oils, sweets
eat seldom
Dairy
2 servings
Meat, Fish, Beans
2 servings
Vegetables
3 servings
Fruits
2 servings
Grain
Group
6 Servings

"It's important to eat a healthy diet. Each food group has different nutrients that our bodies need to grow and function properly. There are five food groups that you should know about. Fats and oils are one of the food groups, but you should limit how much you eat from this group. This group includes things like fast foods from drive-through restaurants, french fries, burgers, deep-fried foods, candy, soda, chips, sugary desserts, and other foods high in fats and sugars. Excessive foods from this group can be bad for your health.

"Another group is the protein group which includes foods like red meat, chicken, fish, dry beans, eggs, and nuts. Proteins help us to grow and repair our bodies as well as provide vitamins and minerals. The dairy group includes foods like milk, cheese, and yogurt. This group provides the calcium and vitamins we need for strong bones, teeth, and other body functions. The fruits and vegetable groups provide vitamins, minerals, and antioxidants that support our immune system. The last group is the carbohydrates or grain group which includes foods like rice, pasta, bread, noodles, corn, and oats. These foods are important because they give us energy. It's also important to drink plenty of water to hydrate all parts of our bodies."

Exercise 60 mins per day

"Exercise helps to develop healthy bones, muscles, and joints. It promotes increased strength and control of our body. Exercise can help keep us from becoming overweight, improve our flexibility, and improve our balance. This is also important for brain health to promote learning, manage mood, and boost energy levels. Exercise strengthens our heart and lungs as well as improves and maintains other body functions.

"Our bones do most of their growing when we are young. Along with a healthy diet, it's important to try to get sixty minutes of exercise each day at our age. Adults should get an average of three hundred minutes per week (or five hours per week) to stay in shape. Building healthy bones and bodies when we are young will help prevent a lot of health problems when we get older.

"We can get exercise by running, jumping, doing gymnastics, playing on the playground, playing ball, participating in phys ed, swimming, riding a bike, ice-skating or Rollerblading, doing yoga, and many other activities. See how many activities you can think of?"

Protect your skin

"It's important to keep your skin healthy. Your skin is like a protective shield or wall that surrounds your body and what's inside. It is considered the largest organ of the human body. Its job is to keep germs out, regulate your body temperature, and hold all your insides together. Your skin allows you the sensation of touch, so you can experience hot, cold, pain, and so much more. Your skin has many layers, and you will learn about those in health classes.

"If you get a cut or injury to your skin, it is important to clean the wound with soap and water then pat the area dry with a clean cloth. Clean the area with rubbing alcohol or an antibacterial agent. Be sure to have a parent help you. Cleaning the wound well will help prevent infections from happening. Don't pick at a scab because that will reopen a wound and allow germs to enter your body. I need to be very careful not to get infections because of my weakened immune system.

"It's important to be careful not to get sunburned. This, too, can cause infections if your skin blisters and peels. Sometimes, a bad sunburn can cause cancer over time. Avoid the sun between 10:00 a.m. and 4:00 p.m. when the most harmful rays are present. Wear sunscreen to protect your skin.

"Certain plants or chemicals can also blister and burn your skin along with fire accidents. Be sure to follow safety rules and check with your parents before handling or being around these types of potential problems. Your skin is the largest part of your body and has several important jobs. Take good care of it. Drink plenty of water to stay hydrated and eat a balanced diet to promote good skin health."

How do you feel today?
Happy
Sad
Angry
Scared
Excited
Surprise

"Feelings or emotional concerns that a child with psoriatic arthritis may experience.

"Having a disorder like psoriatic arthritis can make you feel like you are different from everyone else. You might think that it's not fair, and you may not be able to understand why this happened to you. If your pain or discomfort is left untreated, you may become depressed. Depression often makes you feel sad, tired, and lonely, and you may have low energy. You may develop low self-esteem and feel that you don't always fit in. When playing with others, you may feel clumsy because your physical abilities may be affected. If you and your family feel it is needed, it may be helpful for you to see a counselor who can help you talk about your feelings and better help you deal with this. I know that I can talk to my parents and especially my grandma who knows what it feels like to have this condition. I know that she has it too and that she can be one of the best people in my support group.

"Having psoriatic arthritis is hard to explain to someone because it can be hard to see. People may think you are lying, and there is nothing wrong with you, and you are just seeking attention. When someone breaks their arm, you can see a cast on their arm and know that they may have pain or discomfort. Psoriatic arthritis is hard to see or understand. Some days are good, and some are not so good because symptoms change. You may have stiffness in the mornings and feel better in the afternoon with a decrease in symptoms. When you become tired, your symptoms can become worse. If you have this condition, be sure that your teachers know about psoriatic arthritis, especially your phys ed teacher, so they know that you may not always be able to do as well at physical activities but that you will try your best.

"Taking meds can make you feel like you are different from other kids. Not everyone wants to take medications every day, but I know that if I don't, my condition will very likely continue to get worse. Some people may think that because I have this health condition, I am not very smart. I am smart and do very well in school. Having this condition does not affect your cognitive ability. Some kids can be rude or mean about these things, and that is why I wanted to do this presentation so they might understand a little better. I may not be the most athletic person in our class, but I still like to play and be included in activities just like everyone else. It doesn't matter if we win or lose in games, it matters that we are kind to one another and help each other to be the best that we can be.

"I remember my grandma told me that we are all special and unique in our own way. What is important is that we learn about each other so we can all help and support each other. We can be a support system to each other in our class. Remember, when we treat others with kindness, they will treat us with kindness too. Don't feel that you have to try to make yourself different to fit in. Be who you are because you are special just the way you are. Do you have a physical or mental health need or learning style need that we may be able to help you with or that you might want to share? Talk to our teacher to see if she agrees that it might be good to share, and maybe we can all be better by helping each other."

Delilah thanked her class for being such good listeners.

Delilah decided that she wanted to end by reading her writing assignment to the class about having friends and what she has in common with them. She explained that she was nervous at first about doing the assignment, but after talking to her grandma, she felt better. "This assignment taught me that I do have friends and that I don't need to worry about how my health condition could make a difference. I realized that even though we are doing online learning, we still are like our own little community or family. Our teacher allows us to go into breakout rooms in small groups and do large group activities all together as a class. I am happy to say that I feel that I have been a good friend to all of my classmates and that they have been kind to me. I want to share my letter about my best friend and what I have in common with her.

"My best friend is my grandma. One thing we have in common is psoriatic arthritis. Sometimes we have sore muscles or dry skin, and we both take medicine for this. I am lucky because we were able to make a long list of the things we have in common and what we like to do together. We like to help each other to cook and to bake cookies and cinnamon rolls. We do crafts, do gardening, make flower arrangements, read books, write stories, eat popcorn, watch good movies, shop at rummage sales, go to parks, be silly, and spend time with family. When we go outside, we are able to collect rocks, as well as learn about birds, animals, and nature. Because Grandma and I both have psoriatic arthritis, we can be a support group to each other. My grandma is my best friend."

About the Author

Sue Kleinhuizen grew up on a family-run farm in rural Minnesota. She was one of four children, being the only daughter. Sue enjoyed the outdoors and working on the farm, especially with all the farm animals, many of which became pets. Sue was active in doing the animal chores and assisting with fieldwork. She learned at an early age how to clean the house, do laundry, and cook. Sue has always enjoyed reading books and often stayed up late at night to be able to finish a great adventure the books had to offer.

Much of Sue's life has been devoted to helping children, including being a mother of three boys, a Sunday school teacher, a Cub Scout leader, a day care provider, and a teacher's aide, and working with people with disabilities.

When the last of her children graduated from vocational school, Sue returned to school herself and earned her registered nurse degree. She worked in a nursing home care and then spent the majority of her nursing career working in a mental health hospital. Sue retired early, shortly after the onset of the COVID pandemic. Sue has an autoimmune disorder called psoriatic arthritis, which has compromised her immune system.

Sue enjoys cooking, gardening, quilting, crafting, exploring rummage sales and thrift stores, fishing, and spending time with her husband, family, grandchildren, and friends. She has had a strong desire to write children's books and took this opportunity to explore her talents. Sue hopes to alleviate fears and concerns that children may have regarding various health conditions through her books. This book was written based on a true event. One of Sue's granddaughters was also recently diagnosed with psoriatic arthritis at the young age of seven.